Light Company Thomson-Houston Electric

The Thomson-Houston Electric Light Company

1110-1116: Noble Street, Philadelphia

Light Company Thomson-Houston Electric

The Thomson-Houston Electric Light Company
1110-1116; Noble Street, Philadelphia

ISBN/EAN: 9783337270452

Printed in Europe, USA, Canada, Australia, Japan

Cover: Foto ©Andreas Hilbeck / pixelio.de

More available books at **www.hansebooks.com**

The Only Automatic Self-Regulating System
of Arc Lighting in the World.

The

Thomson-Houston

Electric Light Company

OFFICE AND FACTORY:

1110—1116 Noble Street, Philadelphia.

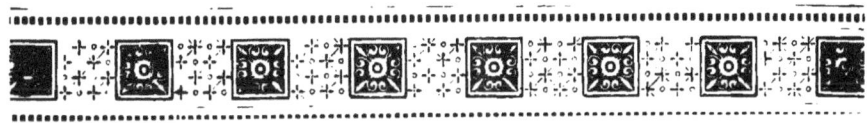

Officers:

O. BAIRD, *President*

J. ... *Secretary and Treasurer.*

L. ..., *General Manager.*

Directors:

SAM W. PETTIT,

GEO W. HILL.

The

Thomson-Houston

Electric Light Company

1110–1116 NOBLE STREET,

PHILADELPHIA.

Philadelphia :
Press of Review Printing House, Walnut and Fourth Streets.
1885.

FIG. 1.

Fig 1 is a perspective view of the machine, and Fig. 2 shows some of the parts in section. The field magnets consist of two

FIG. 2.

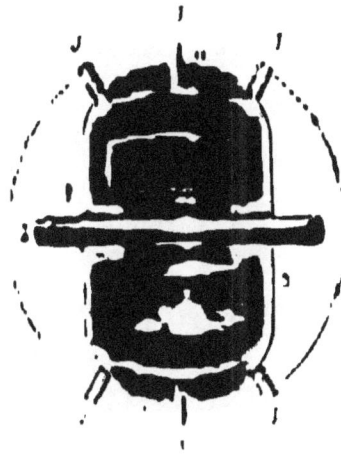

by a varnish of gum lac. Then, commencing at h, one-half of the
first bobbin is wound, the core is then turned 120° and one-half
of the second bobbin is wound. The third bobbin is also com-
menced at h, but is wound full length. Next the second half of

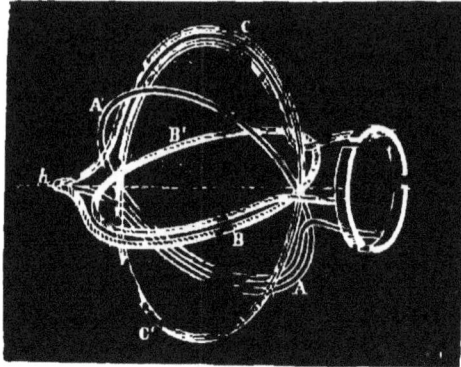

FIG. 4

the second bobbin and finally that of the first bobbin, are com-
pleted, over the surfaces corresponding to their first halves. The
inner ends of the wire connected at h, as stated above, and

FIG. 5.

external ends are carried to the sections of the commutator, the
points at which the various bobbins cross each other being covered
with insulating material. It will also be noticed that the crossing

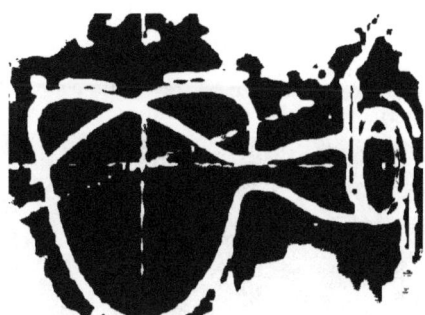

8

place at the instant the latter reaches a point 60˚ from the neutral line ; or, in other words, when it has reached a point at which it is no longer important to gather the current.

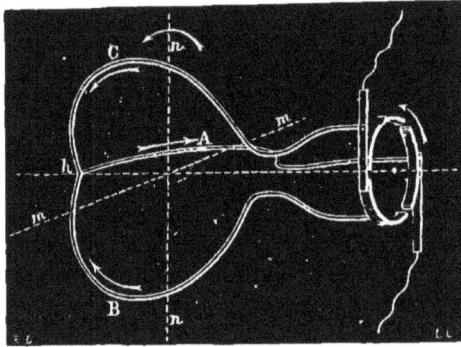

FIG. 7.

Prof. Thomson accomplished this at first by cutting the segments of his commutator so as to leave steps at the ends, Fig, 8, which lap over about 35°. In this way two adjacent bobbins, B and C, for example. Fig. 7, remain in parallel while the armature passes over an arc of 35°, and the currents generated in B during that time are utilized. Another advantage of this arrangement consists in the fact that each brush comes in contact with a bobbin at the moment in which the latter becomes active, and does not leave it until it is almost completely inactive. The spark due to the extra current is consequently considerably diminished.

This form of commutator, although efficient, has been replaced

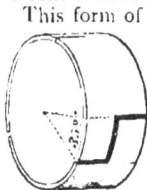

FIG. 8.

by another, in which the segments terminate as usual in simple square ends. The same result is accomplished. however, by substituting two brushes instead of one. Both brushes of each pair are connected together, but the respective brushes are placed so as to touch the commutator at points 35° from each other, which arrangement is obviously equivalent to the first. Our illustration, Fig. 9, shows this in a very clear manner, the bobbins being represented by three straight lines, intersecting the commutator segments.

This figure also shows the neutral and maximum lines in their true position, designated respectively by n, n, and m, m. In the position shown, it is easy to see that the arrangement maintains the bobbin B in circuit up to the point where it reaches the neutral line.

9

Prof. Thomson regulates the current of his machine by varying the position of the brushes with respect to the commutator, and he accomplishes this object in two ways.

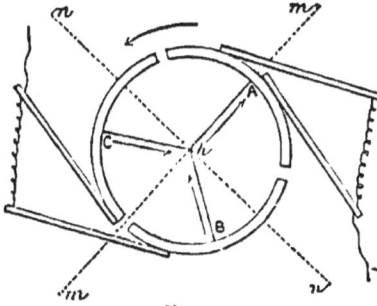

FIG. 9.

The first method, which he terms *forward regulation*, is employed when a diminution of current is required, and consists simply in advancing the position of the brushes a certain distance on the commutator. By referring to Fig. 10 it will be seen that by this means the contact of each bobbin with the brushes is maintained even after it has passed the neutral line some distance. As the current generated in the bobbin after passing the neutral line is in an opposite direction, it follows that, being still in connection with the same brush, it will generate a counter electro-motive force which will tend to diminish the total current. The second method men-

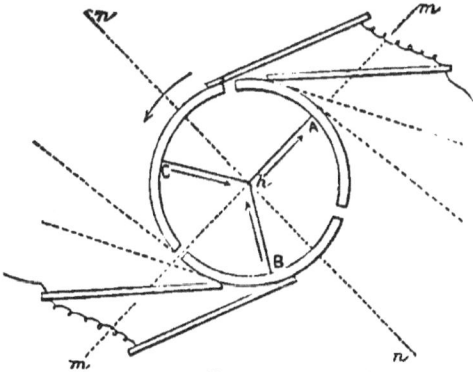

FIG. 10.

tioned above is termed *backward regulation*, and is that which is now generally applied to this machine. Under normal conditions, the brushes in each pair form an angle of 60° between them, and touch the commutator at points also 60° apart, as shown in Fig. 11; consequently the angular distance between the first of one pair and the second of the other pair of brushes is 120°, *i. e.*, the length of one segment of the commutator. It is evident that with this arrangement none of the bobbins will be cut out of the circuit, since each segment of the commutator will have to pass from one pair of brushes to the other at the instant the bobbin itself is at the neutral line; thus there are always two bobbins in parallel, joined in series with a third.

When the machine is working normally, the position of the brushes is that just shown; but when a reduction of the resistance in the external circuit necessitates a reduction of tension, it is accomplished by a peculiar movement of the brushes. In order to accomplish the desired result the brushes *F F'* are given a retrograde motion, while at the same time the brushes *E E'*, Fig. 11, advance a distance three times as great as the former receded, as shown by the dotted lines.

The explanation of the effect produced by this action of the brushes involves a number of considerations; but it is easy to see that if the brushes are spread apart, as shown by the dotted lines, then the angular distance between the pairs is less than 120 degrees. It follows, therefore, that the armature will be short-circuited six times during every revolution by the successive commutator segments.

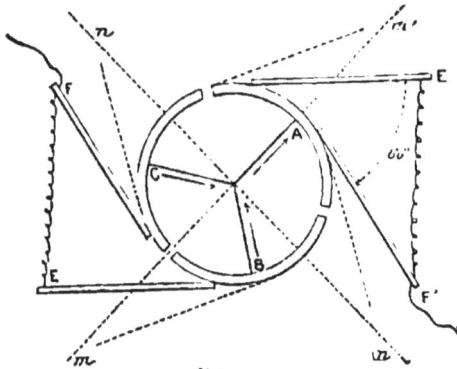

Fig. 11.

At every such short-circuit the field-magnet coils alone are in circuit with the lamps, and it would therefore appear as if the latter would be extinguished or fluctuate at such times. This, however, is not the case, and is explained by the supposition that either the self-inductive action of the magnet coils or the reaction coming from the armature furnishes a current which is capable of

feeding the lamps during the short-circuit. This supposition seems
to be borne out by the fact that when the field-magnets are sepa-
rately excited the machine no longer acts properly.

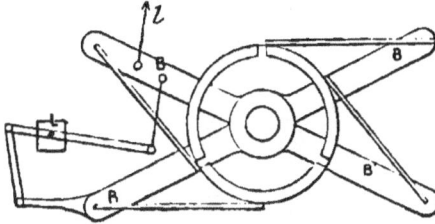

FIG. 12.

The device employed for the purpose of effecting the differ-
ential movement of the brushes is shown in Fig. 12. The brush-
holders B B are connected to those of B' B' by the lever L
vibrating on a pivot so placed that the relative lengths of the lever
arms are as 3 to 1.

This system of brushes is operated by a regulator-magnet,
supported at one side of the frame of the machine as shown in
Fig. 1. The regulator is shown in detail in Fig. 13, and consists
of a U-shaped standard U U, carrying the armature A at its lower
end. The end of the core of the electro-magnet is in the shape

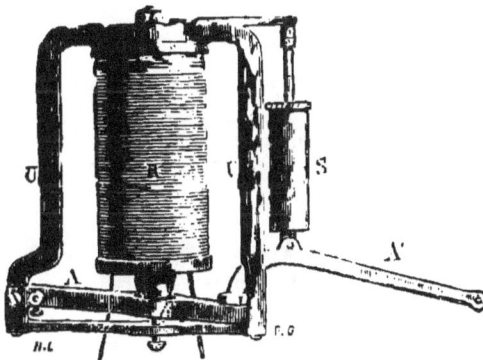

FIG. 13.

of a parabola and enters a corresponding cavity in the armature.
The proportions are such that the attraction is constant for a given
current in every position of the armature within the limits of its
movement. The armature has a prolongation A' which transmits
its motion to the brush-holders by means of the rod l, Fig. 12.
The dash-pot S prevents any violent motion of the lever A'.

If the main current were allowed to pass directly through the magnet R it would act as a regulator, but its action, as such, would not be sensitive enough. For this reason the current is, in addition, passed through a pair of helices C C, Fig. 14, the cores of which

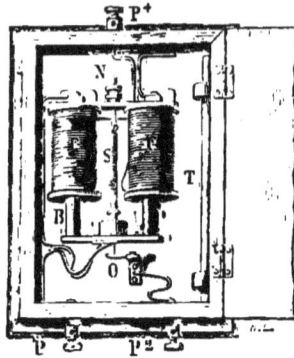

FIG. 14.

are suspended by a spring S. When the current is of normal strength the cores rest upon a finger at O, which contact completes a shunt of no resistance around the electro-magnet R, and the

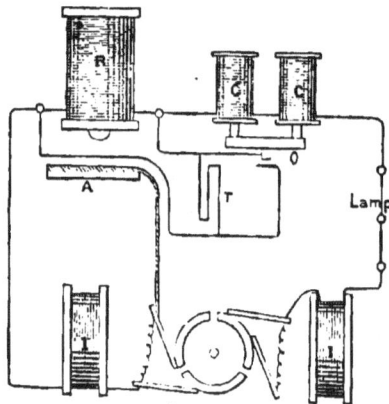

FIG. 15.

latter consequently remains inoperative. If the current becomes too strong, however, the helices draw their cores upward and break the contact at O, which sends the current through R, and

13

causes *A* to move the brushes accordingly. In order to prevent sparking at *O*, a carbon resistance *T* is shunted around it, as shown in Fig. 15, which shows the general arrangement of the entire circuit. In actual practice the cores keep up a continuous movement and effect thè regulation as the variations are produced. The Thomson machine works at high potentials, and when oil is to be used on the commutator for diminishing the friction it is noticed that this oil facilitates the passage of the current under the form of an arc from one pole to the other.

Prof. Thomson has introduced into his machine an ingenious

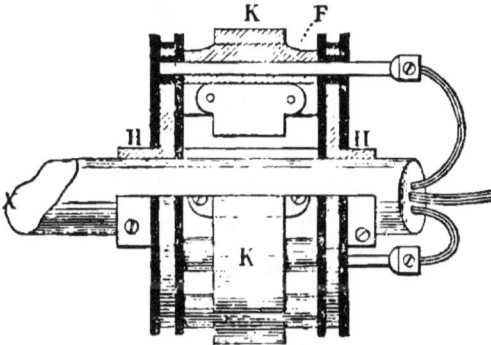

Fig. 16.

device for the purpose of preventing the formation of such arc. He has found that in order to accomplish this a thin blast of air directed against the commutator suffices, and that it possesses the additional advantage of permitting the commutator to be freely oiled. Fig. 16 shows the commutator partly in section, while Fig.

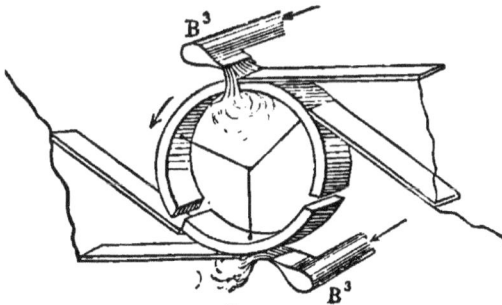

Fig. 17.

17 illustrates the method of applying the air-jets, the two nozzles *B³ B³* being placed opposite to the ends of each forward brush.

In the normal position of the brushes a small spark is produced at
the ends of the commutator segments, against which the air-blast
is directed preventing any injurious action on the former.   The
blower which furnishes the puffs of air is illustrated in detail in
Fig. 18, which shows a transverse section of it.   The hub D is

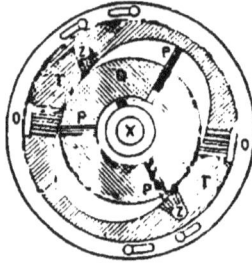

FIG. 18.

mounted on the shaft X and revolves in the centre of an elliptical
chamber contained in the piece T, which is supported by the
frame of the machine.   The hub has three radial slots in which
the wings of hard rubber P P P slide freely.   During the rapid
revolution of the axis the wings are kept against the sides of the
oblong chamber and push the air before them, acting in the same
manner as a rotary air-blower; O O are the air inlets and Z Z are
are the outlets which are connected to the nozzles above the commutator.   The inlets are covered with wire gauze to prevent the
entrance of dust particles, and the hub D is fixed on the shaft in
such a position that the jet of air shall be strongest at the moment
in which the edges of the commutator pass under the brushes.

Special Features of the Thomson-Houston Arc Lamp.

The peculiar mechanism of this lamp, combining a number of unique mechanical adaptations, accomplishes a result in the regulation of carbons for light without the use of clock-work or dash-pots with liquids, as oils and glycerine, liable to be spilled when the lamp is inverted or turned on its side. The feeding of the carbons is effected in a gradual way, and the light is automatically extinguished when the carbons are completely burned, thus preventing injury to the carbon-holders. Lamps used upon long circuits are supplied with an automatic safety circuit preserving device, acting only in case of accident to its particular lamp.

Hand switches are provided to extinguish and relight the lamps.

The lamps are adjusted to give an arc of such length as has been found in practice to yield the largest amount of light for the least expenditure of power, there being a considerable separation or space between the ends of carbons of the lamps.

The character, color, and steadiness of the light are unequalled.

The different styles of lamps are represented herewith, Fig. 19 being that of the standard single lamp, Fig. 20, that of the standard double lamp; Fig. 21 is that of the ornamental lamp. All of these can be made of any desired candle power, although those of 2000 C. P. and 1200 C. P. are the ones most frequently used.

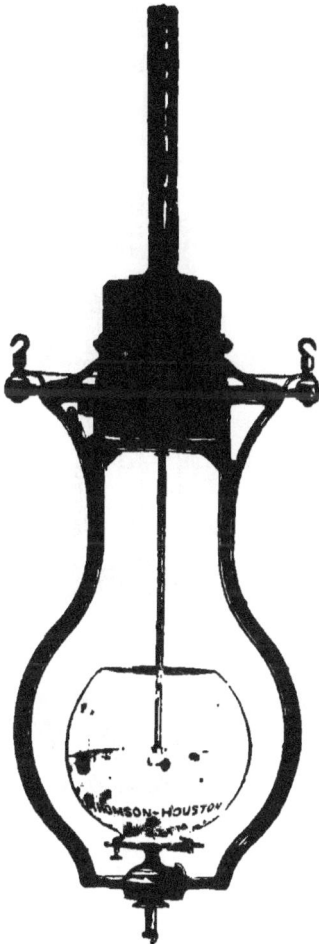

FIG. 19.

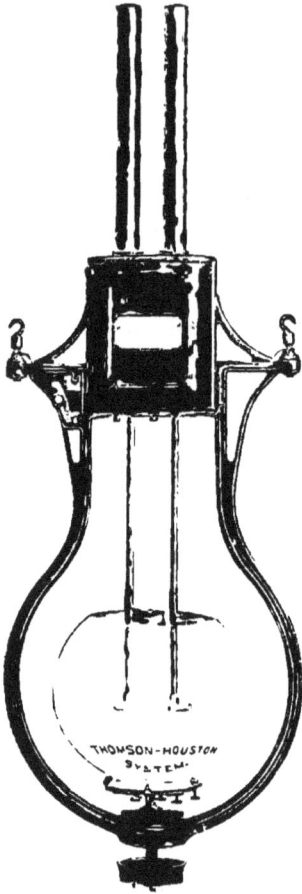

FIG. 20.

FIG. 21.

Importance of the Automatic Current Regulator.

In situations where it is desired to economize motive power, and when more lights are required at some hours of the day or portions of the year than at others, it becomes important not to be compelled at all times to burn all the lights which a generator can supply, but to be able to extinguish those lights not needed, and thus save to power and carbons in proportion to the number of unused lamps.

It is essential, also, that the accidental extinguishment of some of the lamps, or the partial short circuiting of the circuit when by accident, should not result in burning the armature or commutator, thus requiring its renewal at considerable expense.

Generators have frequently been seriously damaged from such cause when no automatic regulation has been provided.

Another point of great importance to the purchaser is that the system should be so perfect that the quantity and steadiness of light furnished will be unaffected by increase of speed or change in the motive power, so as not to prevent coupling the generator to the ordinary engine or water power driving the other machinery of a mill.

This perfection is attained only with the Thomson-Houston regulator.

It is, of course, preferable to drive the lighting machinery by special power, but it should not be essential to devote a special engine exclusively to this purpose. Where a very large number of lights are to be worked, special power is, of course, always advantageous.

As a remarkable instance of variations of speed not being fatal to success with the Thomson-Houston system, it may be mentioned that a Thomson self regulating generator has been placed on a mill upon power giving variations of speed from 700 revolutions to 1,300 revolutions at short intervals, and the lamps were not injured, steadiness and brilliancy at all times, and were accepted as perfectly satisfactory by the purchasers.

To users of electric machinery in towns an important saving is effected by permitting the consumer to shut off his lights when he is ready to close his place of business; and for theatres, halls, etc., it is both a great convenience and saving to be able to put out, at will, any or all of the lights, especially when such lights are rented according to the time of use.

The adoption of the Thomson-Houston self-regulating system by local companies in cities and towns, therefore, permits the profitable conduct of business under terms and conditions not permissable in other systems.

The Incandescent Distributor.

We have developed and are introducing a system of Incandescent Electric Lighting by which incandescent lights in groups can be successfully run from the same circuit of arc lights. Hitherto a possibility that the breakage of one or two incandescent lamps of a group might result in the further breakage and disruption of an entire circuit, has prevented lighting companies from a general use of any such method, although some attempts have been made. Our new improvements provide perfect safeguards against any trouble from accidental breakage of a lamp or other unforseen cause.

By an automatic device in the arc light current a group of eight 16-candle power, or nine 12-candle power lamps, can be substituted for one arc light. All the lights in any group can be used at once or any desired number of them can be extinguished at pleasure as easily as gas-light. The device acts by electrical means, being entirely independent of clock-work, and hence affords no chance for a careless attendant to cause trouble by neglecting to wind up a mechanism. We speak of a *group* of lights, but it should be understood that the lights of a group can be scattered about at pleasure, and may be in various rooms, if desired.

The transfer device by which the current is distributed to a group of incandescent lights is contained in a neat box that can be placed in any convenient part of the circuit, and is known as the Incandescent Distributor.

In this connection we publish the following letters:

[COPY.]

PROVIDENCE, R. I., June 25, 1885.

A. THOMAS, *Supt Narragansett Electric Light Co.*

DEAR SIR:—The incandescent lights of the Thomson-Houston system, as run from distributing boxes, which were placed in our store some time since, has given, it affords us pleasure to say, the utmost satisfaction since their being started. It is our opinion that the lights are fully equal to the best incandescent lights we have ever seen. They seem to exactly fill the want for a good incandescent system which can be operated at a long distance from the central station.

Yours truly,

(Signed) JAMES, KENNEDY & CO.

Boston, July 1, 1885.

Thomson-Houston Electric Co.

Gentlemen:—In answer to your inquiry, we desire to say that the plant of arc and incandescent combined of the Thomson-Houston system applied to our station and yards by the Merchants' Electric Light and Power Company, using your system of electric lighting in Boston, have given admirable satisfaction since they started, and appear to us to be just what is wanted for a combined system of arc and incandescent. We can most heartily recommend them to all inquiries for a thoroughly satisfactory system of incandescent lighting.

Very sincerely yours,

(Signed) J. R. KENDRICK,
Gen'l Manager Old Colony R. R.

Summary of the Thomson-Houston System.

The following is a summary of the features peculiar to the Thomson-Houston system of electric lighting, which is secured to our manufacturing company by patents covering the entire system:

1. A spherical armature.

2. An armature enclosed by the field magnet coils for increasing effectiveness.

3. An armature coil system, consisting of three branches, the simplest winding possible for continuous currents.

4. A commutator of three segments, the simplest in the world, giving continuous currents.

5. Air space all around commutator segments, giving perfect insulation.

6. Field coils externally cased in iron.

7. Automatic regulator, adjusting the commutator brushes and admittting extinguishment of lights at will.

8. Lamp mechanism without clock-work, or liquids that may be spilled, and effecting a gradual feeding of the carbons.

9. Device for dropping the carbons and extinguishing the light when sufficiently burned.

10. Automatic safety device of novel construction for preserving the continuity of a circuit, and used only in case of accident.

11. Spark preventer and air blast, for simplifying the construction and saving wear, attendance, etc., on the larger generators.

12. Distribution switch, permitting lights to be controlled, interchanged one with another, and changed from one generator to another.

13. Distributor box, permitting groups of incandescent lights to be run from the same circuit as the arc lights.

Summary of well-known Facts concerning the Thomson-Houston System.

The Thomson-Houston system is automatic and self-regulating. These highly essential and valuable features are possessed by no other Company in existence.

Its lights can be turned on or off at will and without attention to the dynamo, thus effecting a corresponding saving of power. This is not possible with any other system.

The Thomson-Houston system has in *every case* where it has exhibited in competition with others, received the FIRST PRIZE for every valuable feature. This cannot be said of any other Company in the world.

At the great Industrial Exposition at Cincinnati, in the autumn of 1883, it received the FIRST PRIZE for best system of arc lighting. At the great exhibition held at Louisville, the same year, it received the FIRST MEDAL for BEST ARC LIGHT. At the exhibition held at San Francisco in the summer of 1884, it received the FIRST GOLD MEDAL. In August, 1885, it received the ONLY gold medal for arc lighting at the London Inventions Exhibition, in direct competition with all the most noted foreign and American systems. In October, 1885, it received from the Society of Arts of the Pennsylvania State Agricultural Society, the first prize, being a silver medal, for the best electric lighting system and machinery. At the most exhaustive competitive test of the various prominent systems ever made by a city, given at Quincy, Illinois, its merits *were fully recognized by a combined committee of merchants, mechanics, and experts.* The result was the award to it of the contract for lighting the city. At the great International Electrical Exhibition at Philadelphia (at which no awards were made), in October, 1884, its lights were pronounced by the "American Gas-Light Journal," *a natural enemy of electric lighting in general,* TO BE THE FINEST AND STEADIEST OF ALL THE SYSTEMS EXHIBITED.

In a letter from Prof. Thurston, of Hoboken, to the Armington & Sims Engine Company, reporting his tests of power required in running Thomson-Houston standard arc lights, he stated that with sixty lights running from two dynamos, the power was but 7·10 horse power per light of 2,000 C. P. each.

From a direct comparison of the Thomson-Houston with other apparatus at the Cincinnati Exposition of 1883 as to the average light in all directions measured, and the relative illuminating power per unit of energy, the jury stated that "there is a difference of **more than forty per cent. in favor of the Thomson-Houston.**" [See *Science*, Vol. III., No. 54, p. 184.]

At no city in the United States has it ever competed for city business that it has not been awarded the city contract. **This cannot be said of any other Company in the United States.**

In many cities in various parts of the United States, particulars concerning which can be had by application, *entire plants of other systems* have been thrown out and the Thomson-Houston installed in their place, thus fully corroborating what is claimed for it, viz : that it is cheaper to PURCHASE Thomson-Houston lamps and dynamos than to operate any other system AS A GIFT.

The Thomson-Houston Electric Company, during the past year, has installed *by far* a greater number of local company plants, in different parts of the United States, THAN ALL OTHER ELECTRIC LIGHTING COMPANIES COMBINED. In proof of which, attention is called to the accompanying list of local companies operating its system, nearly all of which have been organized *within the past eighteen months.*

For testimony with reference to the extraordinary merits of this system, we are permitted to refer to such eminent and trustworthy authorities as Prof. Sylvanus Thompson, of England ; Rowland R.

22

Hazard, Esq., president of the Gramme Electric Company, of New York; *The Electrical Review*, of New York; *The Electrical World*, of New York, or to any of the local companies using its system, and especially to those that have been the longest operating it, such as the Kawsmouth Electric Light Company, of Kansas City, Mo., operating nearly 300 lights; the Thomson-Houston Electric Light Company, of St. Louis, operating 300 lights; the Merchants' Electric Light and Power Company, of Boston, operating 600 lights; the Syracuse Electric Light Company, operating 250 lights; the New Haven Electric Company, 200 lights; the Worcester Electric Light Company, 250 lights; the Pacific Thomson-Houston Electric Light Company, 150 lights, and every other company using our system.

Cost of Electric Lighting in Factories, etc.

The following estimates of the cost of electric light compared with gas at $2.00 per thousand feet, and based upon floor space lighted, will assist in arriving at a just idea of the economy of the new illuminant. The following estimate is based on the use of 40 arc lights of 2,000 candle-power each, each light being employed to illuminate 1,200 square feet floor space, in which case a strong lighting is obtained:

Cost of thirty-five horse power per hour (120 lbs. coal, water, etc.), ...	$0.20
Carbons, ½ cent per hour, 40 lamps, ...	.20
Interest on plant, assuming five hours' daily use, 300 days .	.25
Wear and tear, attendance, oil, waste, etc., five hours' daily use, 300 days, ...	.55
Total cost per hour, ...	$1.20

This will light, in round numbers, floor space of about 150×300 feet, or a very much larger space, where less light is needed. Not less than 400 to 600 six-foot burners would be required to give a very moderate illumination of the same space. Taking the lower estimate:

								Per hour.
400 burners×6 ft.=2,400 ft. @ $2.00 per thousand,						. . . .	$4.80
"	"	"	"	"	1.00	"		2.40
"	"	"	"	"	.50	"	. . . .	1.20

In one year, say of 300 working days, used five hours daily, the saving *directly*, in dollars and cents, omitting the extra quality and quantity of work received, will amount to $5,385 per year, with gas at $2.00 per thousand ; and with gas at $1.00 per thousand, $1,785.

When the lights are used more than five hours daily, the time assumed above, the economy of electric light will be greatly increased, as the items for interest, attendance, etc., per hour will fall in proportion.

Parties manufacturing their own gas, in estimating its cost, must add to it the interest and wear and tear on their entire plant (including attendance, etc.), to make a just comparison with the figures we give as the cost of electric lighting.

Testimonials
From Local Companies and Individuals
Using Thomson-Houston Apparatus.

Mr. William Widlund, to whom many of the following communications are addressed, having been granted by the Peruvian government the exclusive right of introducing electric lights into the eight principal cities of that country, for a period of twenty years, came to the United States with a view of thoroughly investigating the various systems of lighting here. After five months spent in visiting different cities, and making an exhaustive investigation of other systems, he was forced to the conclusion that the Thomson-Houston light was superior to any in the market, and consequently the proper one for him to adopt. Acting upon this decision, Mr. Widlund immediately entered into arrangements with us to furnish all the electric lights for Peru for the full period of twenty years.

These letters are confined strictly to facts, and being an unbiased expression of opinion on the part of those using our lights, are the best evidence that can be offered respecting the reputation and standing of the Thomson-Houston system.

SYRACUSE ELECTRIC LIGHT AND POWER COMPANY.

SYRACUSE, N. Y., March 26, 1885.

Mr. William Widlund.

DEAR SIR:—Yours of the 24th inst. is at hand, and would say in reply that we are so well pleased with the operation and many points of commercial advantage connected with the Thomson-Houston system, that we take pleasure in answering your inquiries at length, hoping we may save you the trouble of unsatisfactory and expensive experiment.

We have tried in Syracuse most of the systems of electric lighting now in use in the United States, including the "Brush," "Fuller," "Parker," or "Remington," "Sperry," etc., none of which gave satisfactory results either commercially or as regards steadiness and purity of light.

The Thomson-Houston was introduced here at a period when everybody had become disgusted with the flickering and failures of electric lights, and at once began to grow in public favor until their strongest competitor, the Brush-Swan Company, *finally withdrew.*

We have now a contract for lighting the city for three years, which was awarded us at higher prices than our competitors, after a thorough investigation of systems in use in other cities. In regard to this matter I should like to have you write to Mayor Thomas Ryan, who made very thorough work of the investigation.

As to the satisfaction it gives our mercantile customers, we have many who depend upon us entirely for light, and use no other illuminant, at the same time paying us from twenty to thirty per cent. more than they formerly paid for gas. though of course they get much more and a better light. These. together with our city lights, yield a large net income, which we are putting into additional plant of the Thomson-Houston system, which is, perhaps, as good evidence as can be given of our confidence in the system.

In regard to economy of running expense. we are satisfied that no system can be properly run with less attendance or power, or so little repairs or danger of accidental interruption of the lights.

If time will permit, you might communicate with our vice-president, Mr. Butier. who lost money on the "Fuller" system, or Mr. W. K. Pierce, who is well acquainted with the "Brush" scheme.

If there is any further information you desire which is in our power to give, we shall be pleased to assist you.

Yours respectfully,

F. H. LEONARD, *Manager.*

THE NEW HAVEN ELECTRIC LIGHT COMPANY.

NEW HAVEN, CONN., March 27, 1885.

To Mr. William Widlund, Boston, Mass.

DEAR SIR:—Yours of the 24th is just received. We are now using the Thomson-Houston system for street lighting, also for commercial lights.

We can say that it is simply perfect. We formerly used the United States, or the New England Weston system, which after a trial of one and a half years, we discarded, as it was a poor light, very unsteady, expensive to run, and there was so much wear and tear, that it wrecked our company.

Those of us who had some faith in electric lighting, formed a new company, using the Thomson-Houston Company's system.

We started our lights December 1, 1883, and have earned *over sixteen per cent. net per year* on our capital.

I can also say that before we took hold of this system, I personally examined every system in the country, going into every State east of the Mississippi river on a pleasure trip, and whenever I remained over night in a city where electric lights were used, I spent my evenings in their stations, getting all the information possible in regard to cost of running, etc.

I found the actual cost to produce lights with the Thomson-Houston system was about twenty-five per cent. less than by any other, and the lights were much better.

We think it is perfection, as do all our customers.

It is the only system which I have seen where the lights burn without a flicker.

Should your busiuess bring you this way, I would very much like to have you call; we will gladly give you all our experience and will show you a nice station.

Very truly yours,

F. A. GILBERT, *President.*

MUNICIPAL ELECTRIC LIGHT COMPANY,
Executive Offices, 104 Broadway.

BROOKLYN, N. Y., March 26, 1885.

William Widlund, Esq., Boston, Mass.

DEAR SIR:—In reply to yours of the 24th inst. in reference to our company using the Thomson-Houston electric system, and with what results, would say that the system was selected by our company after having spent much time and money investigating the various lights brought to our notice, and we can cordially and frankly say that we have never had cause to regret such selection, for in the matter of steadiness of light, economical and satisfactory working order of dynamo, lamps, and the marvelous certainty of the automatic regulator, we think that no light yet presented to the public can compare with it. We have been running one hundred and forty lights from an old-style Armstrong engine, which is used every day, furnishing power to a large factory, and have only lost twenty minutes in six months' run; said delay was caused by a fire in said factory.

We are now building a new station, sixty by one hundred feet, with five engines and facilities for six hundred lights, and shall most certainly give the order to the Thomson-Houston Electric Company for all electrical apparatus needed to complete the same.

You will find that it will *cost you less to run their system than any other in the market*, and that the saving in the point of attendance and power used, and repairs in lamps and dynamos, would amount to a very large interest on the entire cost of plant. The Thomson-Houston Electric Company and their people were entire strangers to us when we were investigating the matter of choice of systems, but have found them to be as good as their system, which is saying a great deal, when we are of the opinion that it is the best in the world. If you are in the neighborhood of our city, would be pleased to have you examine the station, etc.

Respectfully,

CHARLES COOPER, *President.*

ST. JOSEPH ELECTRIC LIGHT COMPANY.

ST. JOSEPH, MO., March 2, 1885.

Wm. Widlund, Boston, Mass.

DEAR SIR:—Replying to your favor of February 26th, will say that we are using the Thomson-Houston system of electric lighting, which I think cannot be equalled by any other system in the country. There are some features in this system which make it *par excellence* over any other system within my knowledge. The horse-power consumed per light being very low, about $\frac{3}{4}$ horse-power for 2,000 candle-power lamps, and about $\frac{50}{100}$ for the divided arc. The automatic regulation is a feature that can hardly be estimated in dollars and cents. It thoroughly and completely protects the machines and lamps from accidents by a short circuit. Any number of lamps may be turned on or off without any attention whatever being given the machine by the attendant. As lamps are turned off, the motive power consumed is correspondingly reduced. It is my experience that the lights give more universal satisfaction to subscribers than any other system with which I am acquainted. They burn perfectly noiseless and are no trouble to keep in repair.

This company *earned five per cent. quarterly* last year. Three of these dividends were paid in cash to the stockholders. The last one, payable January 1, was set aside. You will observe that we earned twenty per cent. last year, fifteen of which was paid in cash.

Yours very respectfully,

W. C. STEWART, *Supt.*

THE HARTFORD ELECTRIC LIGHT COMPANY

HARTFORD, CONN., February 27, 1885

Wm. Widlund, Esq., Boston

DEAR SIR:—In reply to an inquiry made by Mr. George Widlund I will say that we have been using the Thomson Houston system fo about two years, and now consider it the most economical system for electric lighting extant.

In regard to paying dividends I will say that we have expended several thousand dollars on construction account, and this has been paid largely from the receipts of the lights now running, and in the face of that we are able now to declare and have declared a quarterly dividend payable March 1.

In conclusion I will say that we consider it the best and most economical system in use.

Yours truly,

F. A. FRENCH, *Supt*

OFFICE OF THOMSON HOUSTON ELECTRIC LIGHT AND POWER COMPANY

814 SIXTH STREET, SACRAMENTO, CAL., Apr. 6, 1885

William Widlund, Esq., Boston

DEAR SIR:—Yours of the 24th of March received, and I must say the Thomson-Houston system does all the company claimed for it when I was negotiating.

It cost considerable more for extras than I anticipated, but I am satisfied it costs the Brush people, with whom we are competing quite as much and more for repairs, especially to armatures, as they have burned out several to our none.

We are paid about twice as much for our lights as the Brush company, and in a year we have lost but one customer. It costs a little more to run than the estimate, but coal and labor are n't so cheap here as in the east.

I spent two years' time in investigating the various systems o lighting, and one year ago concluded the Thomson Houston system to be the best. Our company purchased that system, and have no up to this time expressed a regret, and are fully satisfied we have the best and most practical at present used in the world.

Yours very truly,

F. H. WATERHOUSE

WOONSOCKET ELECTRIC MACHINE AND POWER CO.

WOONSOCKET, R. I., March 25, 1885

Wm. Widlund, Boston, Mass

DEAR SIR:—I received your letter of inquiry this morning and will endeavor to answer it, and I hope satisfactory to you. As you state, we "do use the Thomson-Houston system of arc lighting," and have used it for two years, and in the face of strong opposition (as the local gas company is composed of the most influential men of the town), we have built up such a strong feeling in favor of our lights that the town has contracted for some of them to light their streets. In regard to the system itself, as far as we are enabled to judge from experience, correspondence, etc., it is the very best one at present in use in this country, notably for quantity, quality, and steadiness of the light. Providence and Newport, the two largest cities of the State, have discarded their old systems and substituted the Thomson-Houston arc lamps, and are both well pleased with the change.

Since we have started here the citizens have been more than satisfied with our lights, and those of them who have travelled to other cities, where other and different systems of electric lighting are employed, have returned and express the opinion that those in their own town are equal and in many cases superior to those they have seen elsewhere.

The ease and rapidity with which our dynamo throws off its full number of lights and adjusts itself to a smaller number or load, and *vice versa*, with no perceptible change or interruption of the steady current, has always been a source of gratification to us, and cannot fail to commend the same system to others.

I remain, respectfully yours,

LEVI C. LINCOLN, *Treasurer.*

––––

CONNECTICUT DISTRICT TELEGRAPH AND ELECTRIC CO.

WATERBURY, CONN., March 25, 1885.

Wm. Widlund, care Matthew Crosby, 92 State Street, Boston, Mass.

DEAR SIR :—Yours of the 24th inst. received, and in reply will say that before we accepted the Thomson-Houston system we gave the other systems a thorough ventilation, and will say that after looking them over we determined the Thomson-Houston Company's system to be the steadiest, most economical, and reliable of them all, and its use here has been a perfect success, and we take great pleasure in recommending its use to your people. They will not only find it gives the most satisfactory light, but will prove the most substantial financially.

Yours truly,

A. M. YOUNG, *Secretary.*

THE ESSEX ELECTRIC COMPANY

HAVERHILL, MASS., March 25, 1885

Mr. Wm. Widlund, Boston, Mass.

DEAR SIR:—In reply to yours of the 24th, inquiring about the Thomson-Houston system would say that I think it the most perfect and economical system in the market. Consumers who have used in Boston both the Brush and Weston systems in their stores, claim the Thomson-Houston is far superior to either, and I know from my experience that it is the most economical, owing mostly to the perfect arrangement for regulation. I should advise that you visit the company's factory at Lynn, Mass., and there you can see and have explained all the details, and I think you will have no hesitation in saying with me that the Thomson-Houston system is superior to all others.

Very respectfully yours,

D. W. DUNN,
Manager Essex Electric Co.

THE LYNN ELECTRIC LIGHTING COMPANY

LYNN, MASS., February 27, 1885

Mr. Widlund.

DEAR SIR:—Yours of yesterday is at hand. In answer to your inquiry, I would say that we have every reason to be well satisfied with the Thomson-Houston system of electric lighting, because the light gives our customers complete satisfaction, and the stockholders good profits. We have paid a dividend of *seven per cent from the start*, which was the spring of 1882, and have a surplus of $5,000 to $6,000. I should be pleased to have you call down to Lynn, only half an hour's ride, and see our plant, when I can give you any additional particulars you would like to know.

Respectfully yours,

HENRY R. VALPEY, *Treas*

OFFICE OF THE ST. LOUIS THOMSON-HOUSTON ELECTRIC CO.,
No. 323 North Third Street

ST. LOUIS, March 30, 1885

Wm. Widlund, care of Matthew Crosby, 93 State Street, Boston, Mass.

DEAR SIR:—Replying to your favor of the 24th inst., would say that we believe the system of arc lighting controlled by the Thomson-Houston Company, of Boston, to be all that is claimed for it

We have been using it without any serious trouble, and find it very satisfactory. It is undoubtedly the best system of arc lighting now in use.

We have no connection whatever with the parent company.

Very respectfully,

D. R. POWELL, *Prest.*

OFFICE OF LEAVENWORTH COAL COMPANY.

LEAVENWORTH, KANSAS, March 30, 1885.

Wm. Widlund, Esq.

DEAR SIR:—In reply to yours of the 24th inst., would say that we do not believe the Thomson-Houston system of electric arc lighting can be too highly recommended.

Its automatic and self-regulating features, its simplicity, durability, economy, and steadiness of the light, renders it, in our opinion, superior to all other arc lighting systems in existence.

Respectfully yours,

LEAVENWORTH COAL CO.

WACHUSETT ELECTRIC LIGHT COMPANY,

FITCHBURG, MASS., March 28, 1885.

William Widlund, Boston.

DEAR SIR:—Yours of the 24th is at hand, and in reply I will state that we have been using the Thomson-Houston system of arc lighting for the past two years, and we can say that it gives perfect satisfaction, and we think it is the best in use.

Yours respectfully, GEO. W. PINKHAM, *Supt.*

THE SALEM ELECTRIC LIGHTING COMPANY,

SALEM, February 28, 1885.

William Widlund, Esq.

DEAR SIR:—In reply to yours of the 26th would say that this company is using the Thomson-Houston system of lighting with with entire satisfaction.

We have for sale three 10-light Weston machines and lamps. Price, $600 for each machine and 10 lamps.

Yours truly, H. M. BATCHELDER, *Treas.*

LEWISTON & AUBURN ELECTRIC LIGHT COMPANY,

AUBURN, ME., March 28, 1885.

Matthew Crosby, Esq.

DEAR SIR:—Your favor of the 23d inst. reached me to-day. In reply can say that we are running 112 Thomson-Houston arc lights, having been in the business eighteen months. We have found the lights very satisfactory to ourselves and our customers.

I believe the Thomson-Houston system to be superior to any other that I have seen, in perfection of light and expense of running.

Very respectfully,   N. I. JORDAN, *Treas.*

HELENA, MONTANA, July 15, 1885.

H. M. Ogden, Esq., care of Montana Company, Limited, Marysville, Mt.

DEAR SIR:—In reply to your request that I would express my opinion in regard to the Thomson-Houston arc system of electric lighting, I take great pleasure in expressing my entire satisfaction therewith.

Before seeing it I was very much prepossessed with the Weston, but after several months' experience with yours, I am prepared to say that it is the equal of any light in purity, and superior to any in steadiness. When the the light in the shop was switched off we did not know it in the office, and *vice versa*.

The dynamo being self-regulating, it needs no attention, and never had any at my place other than to keep it clean, renew the carbons, and start and stop it. The man who had charge of it knew nothing about it whatever until it was erected and run one day by yourself. Since that time he has run it without instructions from anyone.

I consider that two of your lights are equal to *three of the Brush,* not only as we have them in Helena, but under the most favorable conditions I have ever seen them.

Yours very truly,   B. H. TATEM.

THE BETHLEHEM ELECTRIC LIGHT COMPANY,

BETHLEHEM, PA., September 21, 1885.

Thomson-Houston Electric Light Company.

GENTLEMEN:—In reply to your favor requesting our opinion of the Thomson-Houston system in use by us, would say: We are pleased in every respect, and find that we have the most economical system and satisfactory light in the country. We have had two years' experience, and in that time, twenty-five (25) dollars would cover all repairs to dynamos; from the sixty-five lights in use we have no complaints, on the contrary, every subscriber speaks of the great steadiness and brilliancy of the light. We now light the entire town of Bethlehem with arc lights, and we believe to the satisfaction of every citizen.

Yours respectfully,

[Signed.]   GEO. W. WALKER, *Supt.*

OFFICE McKEESPORT LIGHT COMPANY,

McKEESPORT, PA., September 26, 1885.

E. D. MULLEN, ESQ., *Manager Thomson-Houston Electric Light Co., Philada.*

DEAR SIR :—Having used your system for the past fifteen months in connection with the Brush and the United States systems, we do not hesitate to say, that in our judgment the Thomson-Houston system can be operated at less expense, requires less attention and skilled labor, and by the use of your automatic regulator, it gives the only steady light to be obtained. Further, the C. P. light is much greater, and with all these points in its favor, think it the only practical, commercial, successful system in use.

Yours truly,   McKEESPORT LIGHT COMPANY,

Z. LATSHAW, *Sec'y.*

PLAINFIELD ELECTRIC LIGHT COMPANY,

PLAINFIELD, N. J., September 26, 1885.

Thomson-Houston Electric Light Company, Philadelphia.

GENTLEMEN :—We have received your favor of September 17th, and in reply would say, the lighting apparatus you sold us in June last, has given entire satisfaction to all our customers, as well as to ourselves. We are much pleased with the working of the plant, and really are surprised at the little attention the dynamo and lamps require. We have an engineer and trimmer, who have lots of time on their hands, and are quite sure they could conveniently handle double the number of lights we have, though we cover a line of some five miles. We expect to increase our capacity and you may soon expect an additional order from us.

We consider it an act of justice as well as a pleasure to give this cordial endorsement of your system.

Yours truly,   CHAS. WANN, *Manager.*

LONG BRANCH ELECTRIC LIGHT COMPANY.

LONG BRANCH, N. J., September 26, 1885.

Thomson-Houston Electric Light Company, Philadelphia.

GENTLEMEN :—Answering your favor of 17th inst. in regard to the service of our electric light plant, would say, we feel we have the best lights in the country, viewing them from the amount of light given, the color, steadiness and brilliancy, and the little care and attention necessary for their operation.

They have proved such a decided success everywhere they have been used, the past three months, amongst the hotels and cottages, that the next season will certainly more than double our plant, and we would not consider putting in any other system than the Thomson-Houston, who have more than fulfilled all the claims you have made for it. Yours truly,

J. S. VEGHTE, *Supt.*

THE NORTHERN ELECTRIC LIGHT AND POWER COMPANY,

543 Diamond Street,

PHILADELPHIA, September 22, 1885

The Thomson-Houston Electric Light Company.

GENTLEMEN:—We have now been running your dynamos eight months, and we find them perfectly satisfactory in every way. Our experience has been that they are the most economical and durable machine in the market; they take less power per lamp, require less attention, and we have not been at one cent of repairs since we started.

On commencing business we had one twenty-five lighter and have since added one thirty and two forty-five light machines, and will give you an order for another forty-five light dynamo by the first day of next month. We trust you will have one ready by that time.

Our patrons claim the light to be the steadiest and best light in the city. Before purchasing your dynamos we gave the matter the closest investigation, and our decision has been more satisfactory than we even expected.

(Signed) GEO. W. BOYER, *Pres.*
(Signed) WM. F. PATTON, *Sec'y.*

GERMANTOWN ELECTRIC LIGHT COMPANY.

PHILADELPHIA, October 15, 1885

Thomson-Houston Electric Light Company

DEAR SIRS:—The plant of 50 lights that you put up for us in Germantown is giving entire satisfaction to us and to our customers. The light is brilliant and steady, the machinery does its work admirably and requires but a minimum of attention.

Our investment is proving profitable to our stockholders, even with but 50 lights, and will be more so when we enlarge, which we must soon do. Yours very truly,

GEO. E. WAGNER, *Pres.*

Cities where the Thomson-Houston system has superseded others.

Among the many cities throughout the United States which have discarded other systems, even after the apparatus had been paid for, and adopted the Thomson-Houston, may be mentioned the following:—

Davenport, Ia., Salem, Mass., New Haven, Conn., Portland, Me., Lowell, Mass., Providence, R. I., Springfield, Mass., Duluth, Minn., Newport, R. I., and others. In connection with the latter city, the following letter from Mr. W. B. Hosmer, a director in the Newport Illuminating Company, and also one from the president of the New Haven Electric Company, will be of interest, repeating, as they do, the experience of all the cities above mentioned.

PERRY HOUSE, NEWPORT, April 11, 1885.

Mr. W. W. Munroe, Boston, Mass.

DEAR SIR:—In reply to your inquiry addressed to the Newport Illuminating Company, of which I am a director, in reference to the history of the recent change of electric light systems in Newport, I will endeavor to give you a few of the facts.

The United States or Weston system had been in use for some time for street lighting, the city having contracted for fifty-eight lights. The contract expired January 1, 1885, and so much dissatisfaction was felt with the system that an order passed the council ordering the lamp committee to contract with the Gas Company for the ensuing year to light the streets in place of the electric lights.

A few days later the lamp committee met to execute the instructions of the council, and were confronted with a remonstrance signed by the best citizens of Newport, who believed that a satisfactory system of electric lighting could be obtained. The matter was referred back to the council, and after much discussion, the lamp committee were instructed to make the fullest investigation possible, of different systems. Some weeks were occupied in accomplishing this work, and finally a full report was presented by the committee, accompanied by a unanimous recommendation that the city adopt the Thomson-Houston system of electric lighting, and a large increase be made in the number of street lights. The committee stated that they were fully satisfied the Thomson Houston system was superior to any other in use.

From NEWPORT DAILY NEWS, February 23, 1885.

To the Editor of the Daily News.

In an article of your issue of the 17th instant, on the Electric Light controversy, the writer referred to the Weston lights in Lowell, Massachusetts, as still in use, although the Thomson-Houston system had been introduced there. I wrote the general manager of the Lowell company for information on the subject, and hand you herewith his reply.

Respectfully, W. B. HOSMER.

BOSTON, February 23, 1885.

W. B. Hosmer, Esq., Boston, Mass.

DEAR SIR:—Your letter of the 19th instant at hand inquiring in regard to the merits of the Thomson-Houston and Weston system of electric lights. In reply would say our experience, after running both systems for two years, has taught us that no company can afford to use the Weston system, as it would bankrupt them to keep them in repair and running. And again, run them the best you can, you cannot give your customers a decent light or a light they will be satisfied to pay for. On the other hand the Thomson-Houston system can be run at comparatively no expense for repairs, and yet you get a perfectly white, steady light without any hissing —a light that pleases everybody. I never have taken out a Thomson-Houston light on account of it not giving satisfaction, while we have been obliged to take out every Weston light we had in stores (about sixty in all , and replace them with Thomson-Houston, and as a last resort we put the Westons on the streets because we did not have Thomson-Houston lamps enough to fill our orders and could not afford to buy more while we had eight Weston dynamos on hand. We have been trying to sell them for over a year, but could not get an offer. As soon as we put the Weston lights on the street, the superintendent of street-lights and the public generally, began to find fault with them, and there has been so much fault found, and they are such a poor light, so unreliable and so expensive to run, that, at a meeting of the executive committee of this company held yesterday, it was decided to discontinue running them altogether, and a meeting of the directors is called for February 24th to authorize the executive committee to purchase Thomson-Houston dynamos and lamps to replace them. We are ready to sell the eight dynamos and eighty lamps at fifty per cent. off list price, and take our pay in Thomson-Houston dynamos at list price. If you wish more information, I would refer you to the superintendent of street-lights and to our leading merchants who have used and are now using the Thomson-Houston. I will send you a list of them, if you wish it.

Respectfully,

J. Y. BRADBURY, *General Manager.*

Electricity *vs.* Gas.

The former an Ally rather than Competitor of the latter.

Within the past few months, the gas companies have been gradually awakening to the fact that, so far from being a competitor, electric lighting, if properly introduced and managed, may prove a valuable ally to their business, inasmuch as it very naturally creates a demand for more brilliant illumination generally.

It is a peculiar, but nevertheless, well-established fact, that in all large cities where electric lights have been successfully introduced, and established upon a paying basis, there the gas companies are carrying on a more prosperous business than ever before in the history of their organization. This belief has become so thoroughly impressed upon the minds of the officers in several large gas companies, that they have purchased Thomson-Houston apparatus, which they are now using very successfully in connection with their gas. A few letters of recent date from several of these companies we publish below, and we would here take the opportunity of inviting officers of gas companies and capitalists interested therein, to correspond with us with a view to testing the success of furnishing arc lights in connection with gas.

The day for unreasonable prejudice is past, and now, in consideration of the high perfection attained by the Thomson-Houston system, in all prominent cities where a demand for electric lights exists or can be created, the local gas companies should be the very first to take steps toward securing the field and furnishing the lights to such of their patrons as may desire them.

OFFICE OF THE MUSCATINE GAS LIGHT AND COKE COMPANY
MUSCATINE, Iowa, April 2, 1885.

The Thomson-Houston International Company.

GENTLEMEN:—In reply to your letter of March 30th, would say that since the introduction of the electric light in our city, we find that the consumption of gas has increased about *ten per cent. or more.*

The conviction is daily growing upon us that the electric arc light, so far from being a detriment to the use of gas, has increased it without a doubt.

We feel pleased with our investment, and would recommend all gas companies to adopt its use, believing that they will find the investment a profitable one.

Yours very truly,
T. COWELL,
Secretary and Treasurer Muscatine Gas Company.

[COPY.]

OFFICE OF UTICA GAS LIGHT COMPANY,

23 Whitesboro' Street.

UTICA, NEW YORK, July 16, 1885.

J. D. Higgins, Esq., Superintendent Rome Gas Light Company, Rome, N. Y.

DEAR SIR:—We are answering many inquiries like your own, as to the effect of electric arc lighting upon our gas lighting interests. We have been experimenting two years with a limited plant used principally for street and out-door lighting for which it seems generally well adapted. Our experience and observation leaves as in no doubt that the introduction of electric arc lighting here has increased our sale of gas. Truly yours,

H. H. FISH, Treas.

[COPY.]

DAVENPORT GAS LIGHT COMPANY.

DAVENPORT, IOWA, July 21, 1885.

Thomson-Houston Electric Co.

DEAR SIRS:—It will doubtless interest you to learn some particulars of our experiment in the use of your system of electric illumination in connection with gas lighting.

We have now operated two of your 25-light machines for somewhat over one year.

We are lighting the city itself with gas, under contract.

In this union of electricity with gas, our company was the pioneer, and despite the warnings and forebodings of our associates, the experiment has turned out an entire success.

Your lights have not only given our customers entire satisfaction, but many of them are almost enthusiastic in their expression of approbation.

We have found your system safe, easy, and economical in operating, and it is difficult to see wherein it can be improved.

There is one result of our experiment with electricity, which should commend itself to gas companies generally, and that is its tendency to increase the consumption of gas. This is easily explained by the fact that it educates the eye up to a higher standard of illumination.

Customers not using the electric light endeavor to vie with its greater brilliancy by burning gas at full head, and this increases their consumption.

Thus among our large consumers, we have a capacious and popular hotel. The proprietor, over a year since, displaced gas in the office and corridors with electricity, using five of your arc lights. The curious and important result is, that the consumption of gas in the remainder of his house is larger than his entire consumption before adopting the electric light.

I must not omit to mention that while our adoption of electricity as part of our system of illumination has not decreased our gas profits, there is a fair prospect that the experiment itself will turn out remunerative.

If the system continues to work in the future as in the past, we shall easily be able to make as large, if not larger, dividends upon our electric light, as upon our gas plant.

Very truly yours,

CHAS. E. PUTMAN, *Prest.*

The following gas companies have purchased Thomson-Houston Electric Light apparatus and are running the same very successfully in connection with their gas works:

Name of Company.	Location	N L.
The Muscatine Gas Light Co.,	Muscatine, Iowa,	2;
Davenport Gas Light and Coke Co.,	Davenport, "	5c
Twin City Gas Light Co.,	La Salle, Ill.,	5c
Freeport Gas Light and Coke Co.,	Freeport, "	6c
Oakland Gas Light and Coke Co.,	Oakland, Cal.,	7:
Ashland Gas Light Co.,	Ashland, Pa.,	5c
Leavenworth Coal Co.,	Leavenworth, Kan.,	10.

Testimonials.

BALDWIN LOCOMOTIVE WORKS.
PHILADELPHIA, July 26, 1882.

The Thomson-Houston Electric Light Co.

GENTLEMEN :—We have had in use in our erecting shop since October last your system of arc lights. One of your 18-light dynamo machines is employed, and is driven by a special engine which is used expressly for driving three dynamo machines of three different systems of electric light. The light has given us good satisfaction and answered our purpose well. We have found no difficulty in keeping it in order and obtaining from it constant service. We have run most of the time twenty and twenty-one lights on the dynamo, although you have frequently reminded us that eighteen good lights was the capacity of the machine, and that with a larger number we could not expect such good results.

In the latter part of our experience with the lights during last spring we found an improvement in respect to their steadiness.

We have not kept our accounts in such a way as to show the cost of running the light any further than the indicator cards taken from our engine have shown the consumption of H. P. of 15 4·10, including friction for twenty of your lights. This result as to H. P. was not surpassed in the same test by any of the other systems which we have in use. Very truly yours,

BURNHAM, PARRY, WILLIAMS & CO.

Woollven.

EDGE MOOR, July 29, 1882.

Thomson-Houston Electric Light Co.

DEAR SIRS :—We have had one of your 16-light machines running at these works since April, 1881, and added a second one in January of the present year, both of which have given us entire satisfaction. We are, yours truly,

EDGE MOOR IRON CO.

SCHLEICHER, SCHUMM & CO.,
N. E. corner Thirty-third and Walnut streets.

PHILADELPHIA, March 23, 1883.

The Thomson-Houston Electric Light Co., Philadelphia.

GENTLEMEN :—We have just tested your dynamo-machine, running it with one of our 10 indicated horse-power engines, and find it produces eight good-sized lights. We tested engine by brake immediately after the experiment, and the actual power equalled 7 6-10 horse-power. All the other machines tried until now by us, have given two lights less for the same power consumed.

Yours truly,

SCHLEICHER, SCHUMM & CO.

CARLTON HOUSE.

CAPE MAY POINT, N. J., August 2, 1882.

Thomson-Houston Electric Light Co.

GENTLEMEN :—We have now had your Thomson-Houston electric light in operation one month, and I can, without hesitation, say that it gives us entire satisfaction. We think it as near perfect as it is possible to get a light, and it is the admiration of all who see it.

Yours truly,

A. H. HAMILTON.

CONTINENTAL BREWERY.

PHILADELPHIA, July 10, 1885.

Thomson-Houston Electric Light Co.

GENTLEMEN :—In reply to yours of the 8th inst., inquiring as to our opinion of your electric lighting apparatus, we reply that during the time we have used it, since October, 1879, our appreciation of it has steadily increased. Our whole establishment is now lighted almost exclusively by it. and it has given us such satisfaction that upon the completion of contemplated improvements, whereby our brewery will be greatly enlarged, we shall undoubtedly call upon you to furnish us with more apparatus.

Very truly yours,

JOHN GARDINER & CO.

THE FARIST STEEL COMPANY.

BRIDGEPORT, CONN., July 12, 1882.

The Thomson-Houston Electric Co.

GENTLEMEN :—In reply to your inquiry of July 6, the lighting apparatus which you put in our mill gives good satisfaction. The changes in speed in our engine, causing the dynamo-machine to have at times a variable speed, are thoroughly governed by the automatic regulator attached, so that the changes in speed do not sensibly affect the steadiness or brilliancy of the light.

Respectfully,

THE FARIST STEEL CO.,

GEO. WINDSOR, *Sec'y.*

42

THE CHAS. PARKER COMPANY.

MERIDEN, CONN., July 15, 1882.

The Thomson-Houston Electric Co.

GENTLEMEN :—Replying to your inquiry, we have the pleasure of reporting our satisfaction with the working of the three dynamo-machines sold by you to us last winter. We found it possible, when light was not needed in more than a part of our works, to run the twelve-light machine at its usual speed with more than one-third the lights cut off; and the switch-board that you sent enables us to run the lights in our foundry from either machine at pleasure.   Respectfully,

THE CHAS. PARKER CO.,

D. W. PARKER, *Sec'y.*

————

P. & F. CORBIN.

NEW BRITAIN, March, 1, 1882.

The Thomson-Houston Electric Co.

GENTLEMEN :—We have made in our factory a thorough comparative trial of three of the prominent systems of electric lighting, including your own, and have decided to retain the apparatus put in by you. The lights are brilliant and steady, and we find that the automatic regulator allows the twelve-light machine to run any number of lights, from twelve even down to one. By the switch of the lamp we can extinguish as many lights as we please, without any attention to the machine, and without detriment to the other lights in the same circuit, or to machine, and we can switch the lights in again when wanted, with the same facility. This automatic regulation is one feature of your system which, by its convenience and economy, as well as by the protection it affords against damage to the machine and danger from fire, must commend the system to people who are willing to examine the apparatus of all the electric lighting companies.

Respectfully yours,

P. & F. CORBIN.

————

NEW BRITAIN, January 11, 1882.

To whom it may concern :

We can heartily recommend the Thomson-Houston Electric Light, having used it in our store. It brings out the colors of all classes of goods, and lights our store as thoroughly and satisfactorily as daylight.

Any one once using the lights will find it very hard to come down to gas.   Respectfully,

F. H. ALLIS & CO.,

Clothiers, Furnishers and Hatters.

COLD SPRING IRON WORKS.

The Thomson-Houston Electric Co.

GENTLEMEN :—We have lighted our mill by the Thomson-Houston system since October last, and consider it perfection for our work. It has never given us a minute's trouble, and has, we consider, added at least ten per cent. to our product. As we do not use any extra power the cost has been nominal.

Yours respectfully,

MITCHELL BROS.

Thomson-Houston System of Electric Lighting.

The Thomson-Houston System carries off the Honors.

The citizens of Quincy, desiring to adopt the best system of electric lighting, for the purpose of lighting their city, extended invitations to several of the leading electric-light companies of the country to enter into a competitive exhibit of their several lights. The companies responding to the invitations were the Brush Electric Co., the United States Electric Lighting Co., and the Thomson-Houston, and the exhibits were made on the nights of February 5, 6, 7, 8, and 9, with the following result :—

A committee, composed of the mayor, Board of Aldermen, and twelve leading citizens, granted the highest award for quality of light, steadiness, and general superiority, to the Thomson-Houston system of electric lighting.

The general committee referred the points as to strength, durability and simplicity of construction of the machines to a committee of machinists, who made the following report :—

QUINCY, ILL., February 10, 1883.

To his Honor the Mayor and Gentlemen of the Electric Light Committee.

We, the undersigned, machinists and manufacturers, would respectfully report that we have examined the Thomson-Houston, United States, and Brush Electric Light machines, and that the dynamo-electric light machine of the Thomson-Houston Electric Co. is, in our opinion, the best for simplicity in construction and durability.   Respectfully,

M. T. GREENLEAF,
JOHN ROBERTSON,
J. B. RUSSELL.

44

CITY OF QUINCY, ILLINOIS

MAYOR'S OFFICE, February 22, 1883.

H—st n E.. tr Co.,

—At a meeting of the City Council of the city of Feb 19, 1883 the committee on electric light, conHonor the Mayor, the Common Council, and twelve zens, appeared for the purpose of testing the merits of Hick-on Electric Co, the United States Electric the Trost Electric Co reported that the contest t cot day of February, 1883, and upon due investigation as to simplicity of machinery and lamps, It, cost of light, and amount of light, accorded to the Electric Co the greatest number of points. The report of committee was unanimously concurred in.

Very respectfully,

HENRY A. DIX,
City Clerk.

Office of
LILLITHORP & CO., *Limited.*
Post Office Address, *Pittston, Pa*

WILLITTON, July 3, 1883.

Messrs . . Electric Co

—In reply to yours of the 29th ult would say: the machine placed in our works by you in manufacture It has exceeded our expectations It has been in operation it has superseded our works, except in our office where lamps have been placed.
I have only words of commendation for your

Yours truly,

LILLITHORP & CO., Limited.

HER MANUFACTURING COMPANY

TORRINGTON, CONN, June 28, 1883.

—We have had in use for the past year, three of your lamps, and have to say we are much pleased with them and are well satisfied that we get a better light than can be had by any other Expense of repairs has been nothing and the cost of oil very small in proportion to results

Yours truly,

E. A. FREEMAN, *Treas.*

45

OFFICE OF JOHNSON MANUFACTURING COMPANY,
MANUFACTURERS OF GINGHAMS.

NORTH ADAMS, MASS., July 11, 1883.

The Thomson-Houston Electric Co.

GENTLEMEN:—Your favor of the 10th inst. received. The electric lighting apparatus put by you into our works runs to our entire satisfaction. We have had one or two other makes here on trial, but for our purpose your machine is the best of them all. We are pleased to be able to recommend the machine.

Yours very truly,
JOHNSON MANUFACTURING CO.,
Per R. H. SYKES.

RIGGS HOUSE, WASHINGTON, D. C.

C. W. SPOFFORD, Proprietor.

WASHINGTON, August 17, 1885.

The Thomson-Houston Electric Light Co., Philadelphia, Pa.

GENTLEMEN:—After having in use for nearly five years the electrical lighting apparatus purchased from you, I desire to add my favorable testimony as to its merits. I am entirely satisfied we have the best light, not only in Washington, but in any of our large cities, regarded both as to the color of the light, and its volume and steadiness. In this opinion we are joined by the electrical experts here. Respectfully,

C. W. SPOFFORD.

LEWIS S. COX & CO., MANUFACTURERS,

Mills: Dauphin, Eighth and Ninth streets, Philadelphia.

PHILADELPHIA, September 10, 1885.

The Thomson-Houston Electric Light Co.,
1110-1116 Noble street, Philadelphia.

GENTLEMEN:—We take pleasure in testifying to the very great satisfaction that we have had in the use of your lights.

We regard them as being as near to perfection as possible in the point of steadiness and brilliancy; and in the matter of economy, they have proven to us a very great saving over the old method of illumination. But what is of infinite more importance to us, is the fact that, by the use of your lights, we have been able to run an all-night force of hands on a class of work which could not have been made by gaslight. We remain,

Yours very truly,

(Signed) LEWIS S. COX & CO.

CHARLES SPENCER & CO.,

Leicester Knitting Mills.

GERMANTOWN, September 8, 1885.

The Thomson-Houston Electric Light Co.

GENTLEMEN:—In reply to your letter of the 7th, asking our opinion of your system of electric lights.

We have had it in our mill for more than a year, and have found everything entirely satisfactory, both as to the steadiness and brilliancy of the lights, and the general running of the whole plant, and have proved it to be much more economical than gas.

Yours truly,

(Signed)   CHAS. SPENCER & CO.

N. SNELLENBURG & CO., WHOLESALE CLOTHIERS,

40 and 42 North Third street, and S. E. corner Fifth and South streets.

PHILADELPHIA, September 11, 1885.

The Thomson Houston Electric Light Co.

GENTLEMEN:—We have been using a 26-light plant of your system since January last. It affords us pleasure to say that it has been from the start entirely satisfactory, and fully justifies the guarantee you gave us. Our lights are soft, white in color, and perfectly steady. Your Automatic Current Regulator enables us, without change of speed, or any attention whatever to the dynamo, to run from one to twenty-six lights, and the single light invariably shows the same intensity and regularity as any, or all of the twenty-six.

In conclusion we will say, that only those who have thoroughly investigated the various systems and tried them as we have, can fully appreciate the value of these distinctive features of the Thomson-Houston System.

Owing to the steadily increasing volume of our business, we are about to give you an order for a duplicate of our plant for our new building.

Respectfully yours,

(Signed)   N. SNELLENBURG & CO.

The following is a partial list of isolated plants installed by the Philadelphia Branch:

TEXTILE MILLS.

Name of Company.	Location.	No. of Lights.
Chas. Spencer & Co.,	Germantown, Pa.,	33
Lewis S. Cox & Co.,	Philadelphia,	75
Conshohocken Worsted Mills,	Conshohocken, Pa.,	30
Jas. Doak, Jr., & Co.,	Philadelphia,	20
Ellithorp & Co.,	Pittston, Pa.,	14
E. P. & H. N. Almy,	Philadelphia,	13
B. Wink,	Philadelphia,	4

IRON WORKS.

Keystone Bridge Co.,	Pittsburgh,	45
Alan Wood & Co.,	Conshohocken, Pa.,	25
John Wood & Bros.,	Conshohocken, Pa.,	10
Cambria Iron Co ,	Johnstown, Pa.,	25
Baldwin Locomotive Works,	Philadelphia,	21
Midvale Steel Co.,	Philadelphia,	18
Cumberland Valley R. R. Co.,	Chamber-burg, Pa.,	16
A. B. Farquhar,	York, Pa.,	28
W. C. Allison Co.,	Philadelphia,	14
Michael Schall,	York, Pa.,	14
Lackawanna Iron and Coal Co.,	Scranton, Pa.,	14
Pencoyd Iron Works,	Pencoyd, Pa.,	14
Chester Rolling Mills,	Chester, Pa.,	10
Geiser Manufacturing Co.,	Waynesboro', Pa.,	6
American Ship Building Co.,	Philadelphia,	6
Delaware Rolling Mills,	Philadelphia,	6
Edgemoor Iron Co.,	Wilmington, Del.,	32

MISCELLANEOUS.

J. M. Gusky, Clothing,	Pittsburgh, Pa.,	30
N. Snellenburg & Co., Clothing,	Philadelphia,	26
Sichel & Meyer, Dry goods,	Philadelphia,	16
Henry Leh & Co., Dry goods,	Allentown, Pa.,	6
Girard House, Hotel,	Philadelphia,	14
Carlton House, Hotel,	Cape May, N. J.,	10
Riggs House, Hotel,	Washington, D. C.,	12
J. Ullman, Hotel,	Philadelphia,	5
J. E. Ridgway, Concert garden, Ridgway Park, Philadelphia,		20
P. H. Glatfelter, Paper mill,	Spring Forge, Pa.,	18
J. M. Sharpless & Co., Dye stuffs,	Chester, Pa.,	10
Firth & Foster, Dyers,	Philadelphia,	3
Reistine & Co., Printers,	Philadelphia,	8
Levytype Co., Photographers,	Philadelphia,	2
Grand Lake Coal Co., Tow-boat,	Pittsburg, Pa.,	12
Ross & Sandford, Dredge boat,	Washington, D. C.,	2
John B. Stetson & Co., Hat manufacturers, Philadelphia,		20

BALTIMORE & OHIO R. R. CO.

Locust Point, Wharves and Piers,	Baltimore,	50
Camden R. R. station,	Baltimore,	25
Mt. Clare R. R. shops,	Baltimore,	195
Glenwood R. R. shops,	Glenwood, Pa.,	50
Columbus R. R. shops,	Columbus, Ohio,	25
Washington R. R. station,	Washington, D. C.,	12

48

Local Companies operating the Thomson-Houston System.

We publish below a list of the local illuminating companies which have adopted and are now using the Thomson-Houston system. This list is constantly being added to, and at the time of going to press a number of other companies are about being organized, and will soon be in active operation.

Name of Company.	Location.	No. of Lights.
Mobile Electric Light Co.,	Mobile, Ala.,	50
Pacific T.-H. Electric Light and Power Co.,	Sacramento, Cal.,	212
Oakland Gas Light and Heat Co.,	Oakland, Cal.,	75
Bridgeport Electric Light Co.,	Bridgeport, Conn.,	241
Hartford Electric Light Co.,	Hartford, Conn.,	300
New Haven Electric Light Co.,	New Haven, Conn.,	162
Conn. District Telegraph and Electric Co.,	Waterbury, Conn.,	85
Norwich Electric Light Co.,	Norwich, Conn.,	76
Jacksonville Electric Light Co.,	Jacksonville, Fla.,	60
Atlanta Electric Light Co.,	Atlanta, Ga.,	45
Terre Haute Electric Light Co.,	Terre Haute, Ind.,	105
Crawfordsville Electric Light Co,	Crawfordsville, Ind.,	45
Muscatine Gas and Electric Light Co.,	Muscatine, Iowa,	25
Pilcher Improved Electric Light Co.,	Council Bluffs, Iowa,	75
Western Construction Co.,	Burlington, Iowa,	100
Citizens' Electric Light Co.,	Des Moines, Iowa,	50
Keokuk Electric Light Co,	Keokuk, Iowa,	60
Bloomington Electric Light Co.,	Bloomington, Ill.,	175
Mendota Electric Light Co.,	Mendota, Ill.,	75
Thomas Electric Light and Power Co.,	Ottawa, Ill.,	85
Freeport Electric Light Co.,	Freeport, Ill.,	60
Gem City Electric Light Co.,	Quincy, Ill.,	183
Twin City Gas Co.,	La Salle, Ill.,	50
Pontiac Electric Light Co.,	Pontiac, Ill.,	27
Streator Electric Light Co.,	Streator, Ill.,	25
Leavenworth Electric Light Co.,	Leavenworth, Kan.,	100
Western Construction Co.,	Atchison, Kan.,	75
Consolidated Electric Light Co.,	Portland, Me.,	300
Bangor Electric Light Co.,	Bangor, Me.,	114
Lewiston and Auburn Electric Light Co.,	Auburn, Me.,	107
Lewiston and Auburn Electric Light Co.,	Lewiston, Me.,	150
Bar Harbor Electric Light Co.,	Bar Harbor, Me.,	100
Gloucester Electric Light Light Co.,	Gloucester, Mass.,	56
Middlesex Electric Light Co.,	Lowell, Mass.,	300
Lynn Electric Lighting Co.,	Lynn, Mass.,	165
Salem Electric Lighting Co.,	Salem, Mass.,	175
Wachusett Electric Light Co.,	Fitchburg, Mass.,	200
New Bedford Electric Light Co,	New Bedford, Mass.,	150
Fall River Electric Light Co.,	Fall River, Mass.,	200
Springfield Electric Light Co.,	Springfield, Mass.,	136
Worcester Electric Light Co.,	Worcester, Mass.,	300
Essex Electric Light Co.,	Haverhill, Mass.,	100
Jenney Electric Light and Power Co.,	Brockton, Mass.,	175
Merchants' Electric Light and Power Co.,	Boston, Mass.,	600

Name of Company.	Location.	No. of Lights
Union Electric Light and Power Co.,	East Boston, Mass.,	100
Pittsfield Electric Light Co.,	Pittsfield, Mass.,	60
North Adams Electric Light Co.,	North Adams, Mass.,	38
American Electric and Illuminating Co.,	Cottage City, Mass.,	100
Union Electric Light and Power Co.,	Revere Beach, Mass.,	100
Brookline Electric Light Co.,	Brookline, Mass.,	90
Adrian Electric Light Co.,	Adrian, Mich.,	60
Grand Rapids Electric Light and Power Co.,	Grand Rapids, Mich.,	280
Excelsior Electric Light Co.,	Port Huron, Mich.,	100
Duluth Electric Light and Power Co.,	Duluth, Minn.,	100
Kansas City Electric Light Co.,	Kansas City, Mo.,	220
St. Joseph Electric Light and Power Co.,	St. Joseph, Mo.,	100
St. Louis Thomson-Houston Electric Light Co.,	St. Louis, Mo.,	600
Western Construction Co.,	Beatrice, Neb.,	30
Omaha Electric Light Co,	Omaha, Neb.,	120
Lane Spring Hinge Co.,	Asbury Park, N. J.,	45
Long Branch Electric Light Co.,	Long Branch, N. J.,	90
Camden Lighting and Heating Co.,	Camden, N. J.,	100
Bridgeton Electric Light, Heat and Power Co.,	Bridgeton, N. J.,	30
Woodbury Electric Light Co.,	Woodbury, N. J.,	45
Plainfield Electric Light Co.,	Plainfield, N. J.,	45
Hudson Electric Light Co.,	Hoboken, N. J.,	90
Municipal Electric Light Co.,	Brooklyn, N. Y.,	400
Citizens' Electric Light Co.,	Williamsburg, N. Y.,	250
Auburn Electric Light Co.,	Auburn, N. Y.,	103
Saratoga Electric Light Co., limited,	Saratoga, N. Y.,	200
Central New York Electric Light and Power Co.,	Utica, N. Y.,	75
Syracuse Electric Light and Power Co ,	Syracuse, N. Y.,	300
Elmira Electric Light Co.,	Elmira, N. Y.,	28
Rockaway Beach Electric Light Co.,	Rockaway Beach, N. Y.,	45
Poughkeepsie Electric Light Co.,	Poughkeepsie, N. Y.,	70
Newburg Electric Light Co.,	Newburg, N. Y,	45
Citizens' Electric Light Co.,	Akron, Ohio,	250
Champion Electric Light Co.,	Springfield, Ohio,	150
Columbus Electric Light and Power Co.,	Columbus, Ohio,	175
Arnoux Electric Light Co.,	Cleveland, Ohio,	95
Chillicothe Electric Light Co.,	Chillicothe, Ohio.	26
Gallion Electric Light Co.,	Gallion, Ohio,	30
Northern Electric Light and Power Co.,	Philadelphia,	190
Philadelphia Electric Light Co.,	Philadelphia,	50
Germantown Electric Light Co ,	Germantown, Pa.,	50
Norristown Electric Light and Power Co.,	Norristown, Pa.,	50
Ashland Gas Light Co.,	Ashland, Pa.,	50
Bethlehem Electric Light Co.,	Bethlehem, Pa .	80
McKeesport Light Co.,	McKeesport, Pa.,	75
Citizens' Electric Light Co.,	York, Pa.,	90
Frankford Electric Light and Power Co.,	Frankford, Pa.,	63
Narragansett Electric Light Co.,	Providence, R. I ,	470
Woonsocket Electric Machine and Power Co.,	Woonsocket, R. I.,	26
Pawtucket Electric Light Co.,	Pawtucket, R. I.,	50
Newport Electric Illuminating Co ,	Newport, R. I ,	113
Badger Electric Light Co.,	Racine, Wis.,	200
Oshkosh Electric Light Co.,	Oshkosh, Wis.,	60
Janesville Electric Light Co.,	Janesville, Wis.,	50
United States Electric Light Co.,	Washington, D. C.,	270

50

FOREIGN COMPANIES.

Name of Company.	Location.	No. of Lights.
Ottawa,	Ontario,	200
St. Catharine's.	Ontario,	100
Peterborough,	Ontario,	125
Hamilton,	Ontario,	150
Montreal,	Quebec,	350
Quebec,	Quebec,	200
Halifax,	Nova Scotia,	100
St. Johns,	New Brunswick,	100
St. John,	Newfoundland,	90
Panama,	C. A.,	20
Rio de Janeiro, (In course of construction.)	Brazil.	
Para, (In course of construction.)	Brazil.	
Lima, (In course of construction.)	Peru,	100
Callao, (In course of construction.)	Peru.	
Guayaquil, (In course of construction.)	Ecuador,	50
Guatemala Electric Light Co.,	Guatemala, C. A.,	300
	Mazatlan, Mexico.	

www.ingramcontent.com/pod-product-compliance
Lightning Source LLC
Chambersburg PA
CBHW021643270326
41931CB00008B/1146